For my son Edward

A TEMPLAR BOOK

This edition first published in the USA in 1994 by
SMITHMARK Publishers Inc., 16 East 32nd Street,
New York, NY 10016.

First published in Canada 1994 by
Smithbooks, 113 Merton Street, Toronto, Canada M45 1A8.

SMITHMARK books are available for bulk purchase for sales promotion
and premium use. For details write or call the manager of special sales,
SMITHMARK Publishers Inc., 16 East 32nd Street,
New York, NY 10016. Tel: (212) 532-6600.

Devised and produced by The Templar Company plc,
Pippbrook Mill, London Road, Dorking, Surrey RH4 1JE, Great Britain.

ISBN 0-8317-0454-3

Printed and bound in Italy

10 9 8 7 6 5 4 3 2

ALPHABET ZOO

Illustrated by
Stephen Holmes

All sorts of animals fill this book,
Aardvarks and antelopes, zebras too.
So turn the page and start to look.
You're on a trip round Alphabet Zoo.

SMITHMARK

A a

Can you find:
An angry alligator eating an
alarm clock?
An aardvark acting as an admiral?

Bb

Can you see:
A brown bear bouncing a ball
by a bridge?
A beautiful beaver with a basket of
brown bread?

Cc

Can you spot:
A colorful chameleon climbing in
the corner of the curtain?
A cheerful cheetah carrying a
cracked cup?

Dd

Can you find:
A darting dragonfly and
a dancing duck?
A deer drinking from a dish?

TO THE
ELEPHANT
ENCLOSURE

E e

Can you see:
An elephant eating an Easter egg?
An elegant elephant
in emerald earrings?

Ff

Can you spot:
A frightened fox fleeing
to the forest?
A fast frog feeding in the fishpond?

G g

Can you find:
A greedy giraffe gobbling grapes
in the garden?
A gorilla wearing green gloves?

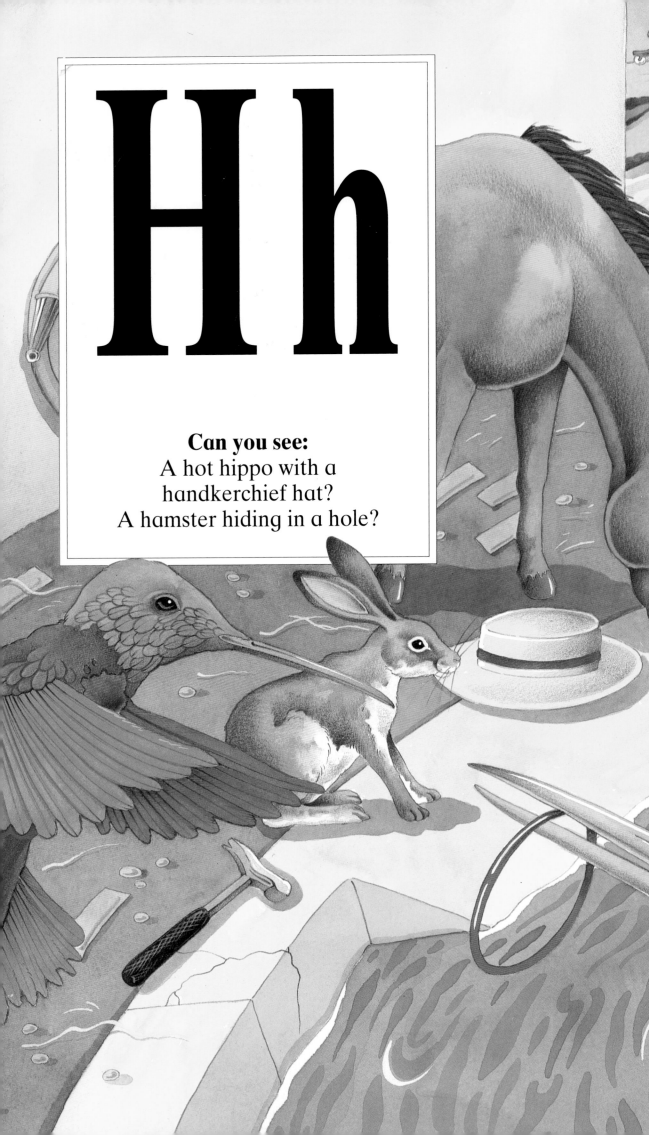

H h

Can you see:
A hot hippo with a
handkerchief hat?
A hamster hiding in a hole?

Ii

Can you spot:
Interesting insects eating
ice cream?
An iron, an ibis, and some ivy?

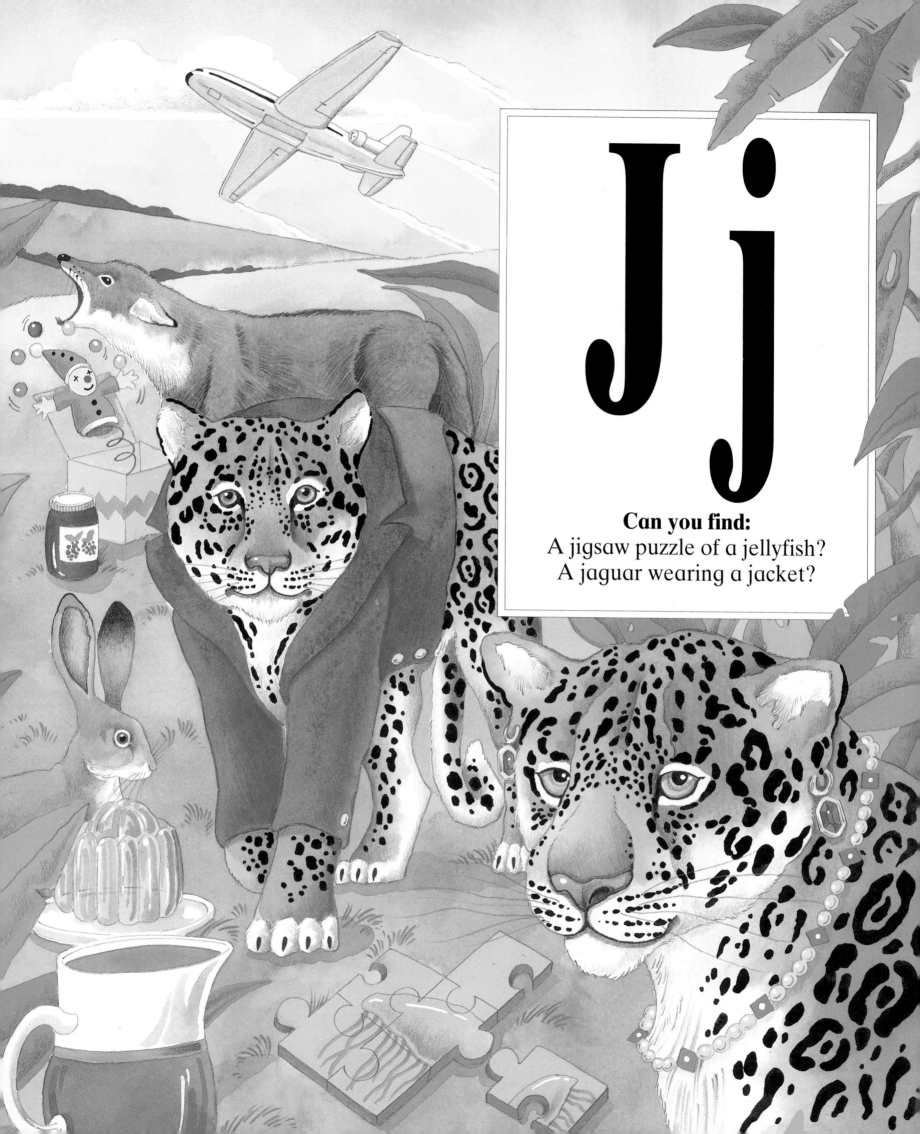

Jj

Can you find:
A jigsaw puzzle of a jellyfish?
A jaguar wearing a jacket?

K k

Can you see:
Kangaroos flying colorful kites?
A kitten with some knotty knitting?

Ll

Can you spot:
A laughing lizard lying on a leaf?
A lioness leaping on a lawn?

M m

Can you find:
A marvelous moose on a
motorcycle?
A mole with a monocle?

Nn

Can you see:
Nine nightingales in a nut tree?
A net, a newt, and a newspaper?

O o

Can you spot:
An ostrich on an outing to an orchard?
An orangutan in orange overalls?

OLIVES

ONIO

OYSTE

P p

Can you find:
A pile of presents by the pool?
A penguin in pajamas painting
a picture?

FEEDING TIMES:
QUARTER TO TWELVE ! QUARTER PAST FOUR

QUIET PLEASE

QUIZ BOOK

Q q

Can you see:
A clock divided into quarters?
Quiet quails by the colorful
quetzal's cage?

Rr

Can you spot:
A rhino on roller-skates with
a round radio?
A reindeer wearing red ribbons?

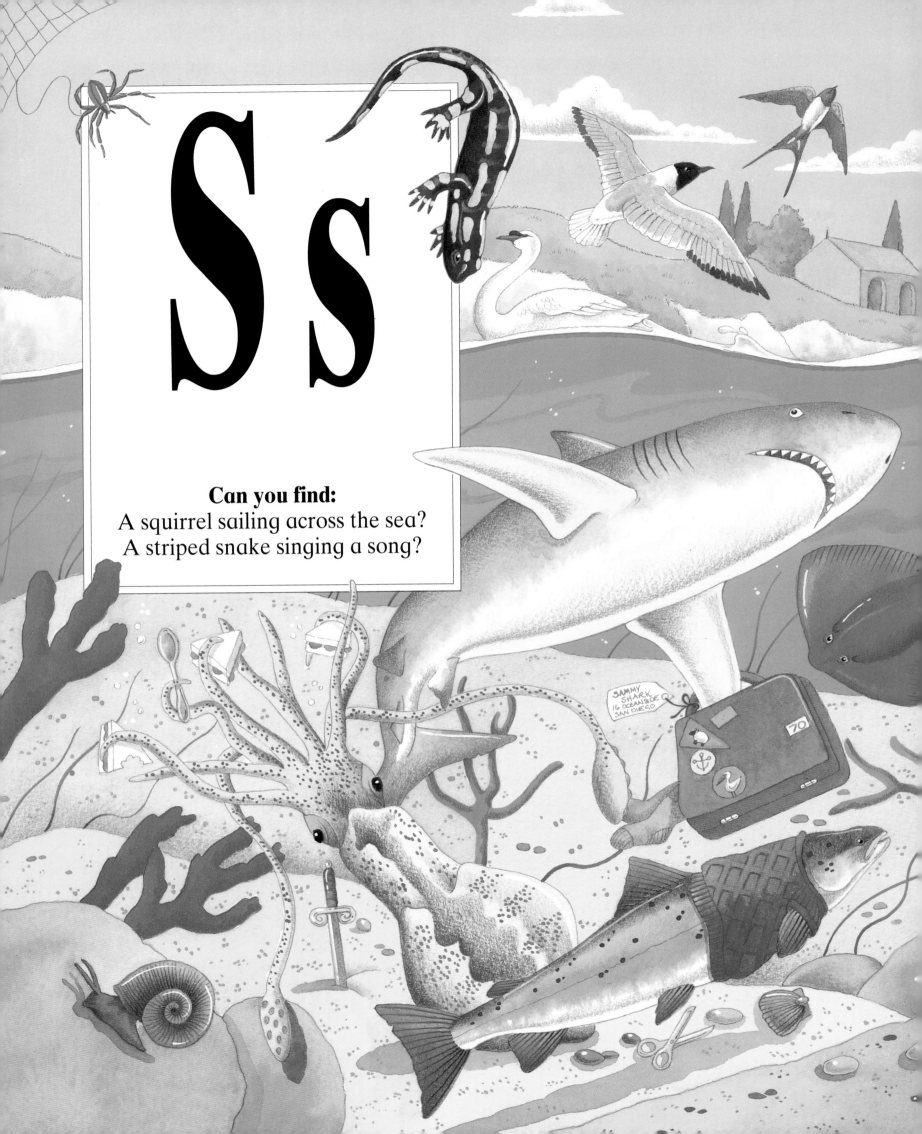

S s

Can you find:
A squirrel sailing across the sea?
A striped snake singing a song?

SAMMY
SHARK
16 OCEANSIDE
SAN DIEGO

T t

Can you see:
Ten tigers sitting at a table?
Two toucans playing tennis?

Uu

Can you spot:
An unhappy unicorn under
an umbrella?
A uniform and a ukulele?

V v

Can you see:
A vulture by some vines?
Vegetables, violets and a volcano?

W w

Can you find:
A walrus in white watching whales?
A weasel water-skiing?

Xx Yy Zz

Can you see:
An X-ray and a xylophone?
A yak with a yellow yo-yo?
A zebra zipping up a zipper?

TO THE ZOO

WORD LIST

Here is a list of animals and objects that you will find in this book.
If you look closely at the pictures you will find that other words beginning
with the right letter are shown as well. For example, on the B page
you might notice that the brown bear is *bouncing* the ball and the
bullfrog is *blowing* bubbles. Look back through the pages and
see how many other words you can spot.

A
Aardvark
Acorn
Admiral
Airplane
Alarm clock
Albatross
Alligator
Anemone
Angel
Ant
Anteater
Antelope
Ape
Apple
Apron
Arm
Armadillo
Arrow
Artist
Aviary
Axe
B
Baboon
Badger
Bag
Ball
Balloon
Banana
Bandage
Barley
Basket
Bat
Beads
Beak
Bear
Beaver
Beetle
Bell
Belt
Berry
Bicycle
Bird
Black
Blue
Bluebell
Boar
Bow

Branch
Bread
Bridge
Broom
Brown
Bubbles
Building
Bull
Bullfrog
Buttercup
Butterfly
C
Cactus
Cake
Camel
Can
Candle
Cap
Carrot
Castle
Cat
Caterpillar
Cello
Chair
Chameleon
Cheetah
Chef
Cherry
Chimpanzee
Chipmunk
Christmas card
Church
Circle
Clarinet
Claw
Cliff
Cloak
Clock
Cloud
Coast
Coat
Cockatoo
Comic
Compass
Condor
Conductor
Cow
Crane (*building*)

Crane (*bird*)
Crocodile
Crow
Crown
Cube
Cup
Curtain
Cushion
Cymbal
D
Daffodil
Dagger
Daisy
Deer
Diamond
Dice
Dinosaur
Dish
Dog
Dolphin
Domino
Door
Dormouse
Dots
Dove
Dragonfly
Drawing
Drum
Drumstick
Duck
E
Ear
Earmuffs
Earring
Earth
Earwig
Easel
Easter egg
Eel
Egg
Egg cup
Elephant
Emerald
Enclosure
Entrance
Envelope
Eye
Eyelash

F
Fan
Feather
Fence
Fern
Fin
Fir
Fish
Fishpond
Flag
Flamingo
Flour
Flowers
Fly
Forest
Fork
Fox
Frill
Frog
Fruit
Funnel
Fur
G
Garden
Gate
Giraffe
Glasses
Glider
Glove
Gnu
Goat
Goldfish
Goose
Gorilla
Grapefruit
Grapes
Grass
Gray
Green
Grouse
H
Hammer
Hamster
Handbag
Handkerchief
Hare
Hat
Haystack

Hazelnuts
Heart
Hedge
Helicopter
Helmet
Heron
Hill
Hippopotamus
Hole
Holly
Honey
Hoof
Hoop
Horizon
Horse
Hosepipe
House
Hummingbird
Hut
Hyena
I
Ibis
Ice cream
Ink
Insect
Iris
Iron
Ivy
J
Jack rabbit
Jack-in-the-box
Jackal
Jacket
Jaguar
Jar
Jellyfish
Jewelry
Jigsaw puzzle
Jug
Juice
K
Kangaroo
Kennel
Ketchup
Key
Kilt
King
Kite

Kitten
Knapsack
Knife
Knight
Knitting
Knot
Koala
L
Label
Ladder
Ladybug
Lamb
Lamp
Lawn
Leaf
Leg
Lemon
Lemonade
Leopard
Life preserver
Light bulb
Lighthouse
Lightning
Lion
Lioness
Lizard
Loaf
Lobster
Log
Lollipop
M
Magazine
Magnet
Magpie
Map
Marble
Marigold
Mask
Mistletoe
Mitten
Mole
Monkey
Monocle
Moon
Moose
Moth
Motorcycle
Mountain
Mouse
Mouth
Mud
Mushroom
Music
N
Nail
Necklace
Needle
Nest
Net

Nettle
Newspaper
Newt
Night-cap
Nightingale
Nut
O
Octagon
Octopus
Olive
Onion
Orange (*color*)
Orange (*fruit*)
Orangutan
Orchard
Ostrich
Otter
Overalls
Owl
Oyster
P
Package
Paint
Paintbrush
Pajamas
Palette
Palm tree
Panda
Pants
Paper chains
Parachute
Parrot
Partridge
Party hat
Paw
Pear
Pearls
Pelican
Pencil
Penguin
Piano
Picnic
Picture
Pie
Pin
Pincushion
Pineapple
Pink
Pirate
Pizza
Plank
Plate
Platypus
Pocket
Pogo stick
Polar bear
Pool
Popcorn
Poppy

Present
Puddle
Pumpkin
Puppet
Puppy
Purple
Q
Quail
Quarter
Question mark
Quetzal
Quilt
Quiz book
R
Rabbit
Racquet
Radio
Raft
Rain
Rainbow
Rat
Recorder
Red
Reindeer
Rhinoceros
Ribbon
Ring
River
Road
Robin
Rocket
Roller skate
Rope
Rose
Ruby
Ruler
Rush
S
Sail
Salamander
Salmon
Sand
Sandal
Sandcastle
Sandwich
Sausages
Scarf
Scissors
Sea
Sea lion
Seagull
Seahorse
Seal
Seaweed
Shark
Sheep
Shell
Ship
Shirt

Shrimp
Signpost
Skate
Sky
Smoke
Snail
Snake
Soap
Sock
Spade
Sparrow
Spectacles
Spider
Spoon
Spots
Squid
Squirrel
Star
Starfish
Stork
Stripe
Submarine
Suitcase
Swallow
Swan
Sweater
Sword
T
Table
Tablecloth
Tail
Tambourine
Tangerine
Teapot
Teacup
Teaspoon
Teddy bear
Telephone
Telescope
Television
Tent
Thorn
Tie
Tiger
Toad
Tomato
Tongue
Toothbrush
Toothpaste
Top hat
Tortoise
Toucan
Towel
Tower
Train
Tray
Tree
Trunk
Tulips

Turkey
Turtle
Tusk
Typewriter
U
Ukulele
Umbrella
Underground
Underwear
Unicorn
Uniform
V
Vacuum cleaner
Vase
Vegetables
Vest
Violet
Violin
Volcano
Vulture
W
Waistcoat
Walking stick
Wall
Walrus
Wasp
Watch
Water skis
Watering can
Weasel
Web
Weeds
Whale
Wheel
Whiskers
White
Windmill
Wolf
X
X-ray
Xylophone
Y
Yacht
Yak
Yawn
Yellow
Yo-yo
Yogurt
Yolk
Z
Zebra
Zig zag
Zipper
Zoo

Aa Bb Cc
Gg Hh Ii Jj
Nn Oo Pp
Tt Uu Vv W